HAVE FAITH IN GOD BUT BELIEVE IN THE DEVIL

GLENN R. THOMPSON

ISBN 979-8-88644-565-7 (Paperback)
ISBN 979-8-88644-566-4 (Digital)

Covenant Books
11661 Hwy 707
Murrells Inlet, SC 29576
www.covenantbooks.com

I dedicate this book to all my fellow sinners in the world. May God bless you and clear the way for you to make it Home.

ALSO BY GLENN THOMPSON

Highly Rated at Amazon with 4.7 stars
Author testified before Congress and testimony
can be seen at the book's website
www.sportofkingsbook.com

Sport of Kings - Book

Jay Cronley, ESPN columnist and handicapper: " Listen, I loved Glenn's book, very emotional
and heart-felt, great job."

www.sportofkingsbook.com

CONTENTS

OBSTACLE COURSE
TO HEAVEN

Strive to enter in at the strait gate: for many, I say onto you, will seek to enter in, and shall not be able.
—Jesus Christ

I want to start this book with a story about a graduating class of Navy Seals. They have been through six months of rigorous training and have one final task before graduation. They have to complete an obstacle course. The course is physically exhausting as well as complicated and deceptive. There are a lot of snags and traps along the way, and the men and women really need to think on their feet. There have been rumors of a wall at the end of the course that is close to impossible to get past! They are urged to consider all choices before them. The twenty men and two women gather at the starting line, and the gun announces the race is on! Off they go with an abundance of confidence and lots of talent to handle the challenge at hand. A mountain is before them, and they need to choose which path to use. They come to a river and need to swim two miles upstream. All in all, there are fifteen challenges ahead of them, and of the twenty-two candidates, many have dropped out by the halfway point.

Finally, after five more hours of extreme difficulty, they come to a fork in the road. The final obstacle, the wall, is now before them, and they are all given a choice. They can run a mile up the hill and take on the wall or they can swim across this large lake and be given a key? As the class gathers and starts discussing the final decision and which path to choose, there are three men and one woman that are leading the conversation. They are very loud and confident and strongly urging the short run to the wall. How bad can it be? We are the toughest and most athletic people in the world! We can get over

1

any wall! Who needs a damn key, and what's it for anyway? We can handle this ourselves. We are the best of the best!

One by one, all but five of the class take off for the wide and easy path to the wall. The members that were pushing this option had a little glint in their eye and were very pleased with the numbers! The five that didn't follow the crowd and chose the lake used a little discernment. They didn't have a good feeling about the shortcut. They also sensed something dark and disturbing about their four teammates. Why were they so confident and blindly pushing so hard? Why no discussion of the lake and the key? Why did they have that look in their eye when most chose to follow them? They ran off in the direction of the lake, realizing that if they maintain a steady pace, there will be ample time to finish the course. Now we get to the wall.

When the "best of the best" made it to the crest of the hill, they saw the wall in the valley. The whole group stopped in their tracks, and all but the four promoters had a sick and empty feeling in their stomach. That damn wall was about an eighth of a mile high! They didn't go running down the hill to attack the wall; for the first time all day, they had a powerful feeling of fear and regret for the choice they made! Some of them thought back to the fork in the road and remembered the strong feeling they had to take the more difficult route and accept the key. They tragically ignored their instincts and followed the crowd and were misled by the four devil's advocates. Sadly, they found comfort in numbers and were getting ready to pay a heavy price for their choice.

The first brave soul walked up to the wall and prepared to do battle. Before he began, he was required to put on a safety harness so that when he fell, he would safely be lowered to the ground. He starts up the wall with an abundance of confidence. The rope has knots in it that make it helpful for his grip and the climb. Up he goes, but a little past the halfway point, he begins to struggle. His muscles start to seize up from the hard day's work, and he falls. The safety rope catches him and lowers him to the ground. His disappointment is devastating like nothing he has ever felt before. He walks away to a small group of trees, sits on the ground, and begins to weep.

Batter number two steps up. He easily makes it past where his teammate fell but is soon to find out that the knots in the rope stop! This makes the climb much more difficult and, shortly, his hands begin to bleed. He struggles valiantly and made it quite a ways up the rope before he sadly let go. Same empty and horrible feeling of loss and regret took over his soul, and he collapses on the ground. One by one, the group goes up, and one by one, they fall. The team leader actually looked like he might make it until he got to the last twenty feet of the rope. He reached up, and his hand slipped down. There was grease on the last section of the rope, and he knew, then and there, that nobody was ever going to make this climb—nobody! Kind of funny, but the four people that encouraged everyone to take the easy route to the wall never bothered to attempt the climb. They didn't need to; they felt their mission was accomplished.

Right about this time, the members from the lake show up. They looked around and saw the sadness and pain in their friends' eyes and were deeply affected! They then turned their attention to the wall. Finally, after a bit of a search, they found a small keyhole in the wall. Before turning the key and opening the door, the five survivors went off to the side and had a private conversation. They then walked over, joined hands with their fallen friends, and walked back to the wall. They refused to go through the door unless their teammates were permitted to go with them! Upon approval, they turned the key, opened the door, and found victory over the wall! The devil's advocates that never attempted the climb were refused the grace and walked away in a search of new prey. Their attempt to cause failure at the wall was defeated with compassion and teamwork.

The obstacle course is the world, and you are in it right now. You make choices every day that determine your future and destiny. You will have many people that intentionally try to lead you down the wrong path. I consider these people to be true advocates and children of the devil. They will be that close friend that will buy you a fifth drink at the bar when they know you have to drive home. When you are having trouble with your marriage, they might suggest meeting an attractive friend of theirs. If you accidentally become pregnant, they will highly recommend an abortion and tell you that it will simplify your life. You are at a difficult crossroad in your life and considering different sexual options. Your friends will pat you on the back and tell you to go for it! Everyone is trying it these days, and it might work out great for you. They will encourage you to cheat, steal, or take shortcuts in your business. They will claim money is much more important than your reputation and talk about a fancy car that will suddenly become affordable.

Just like the four dark individuals in the story above, they will search out any weaknesses you have and exploit it with the intention of sending you down the wrong path, sending you to Hell. These people will come in many forms. Could be your father, mother, brother, sister, son, daughter, friend, coworker, or stranger. When you seriously start paying attention to their actions and intentions, you will soon understand what I am talking about and, hopefully, you will be able to spot and prevent them from manipulating your life! It's very important that you find your true friends in life! Your false friends will tell you not to worry, and your true friends will tell you there are consequences! You will have a large group that will support you because it makes things simpler for them. You, hopefully, will have some genuine friends that are not afraid to hurt your feelings and will honestly try and help! You have a decision to make. Do you find comfort in numbers or would you rather hear the truth? As much as it hurts, sometimes, I like to hear the truth and try not to allow the devil a seat at my table!

Now let's get to the key and the wall. The wall is the gateway to Heaven, and the key is Jesus Christ. Your "friends" that are advocates of the devil will do anything they can to keep you from God! It's their job! There is an interesting quote from Proverbs 4:16 in the Bible. It says, "For they sleep not, except they have done mischief; and their sleep is taken away, unless they cause some to fall." You might be one of those people that don't believe in the devil, but trust me, he is very real, very cunning, and has millions of employees. I feel fairly certain that each and every one of us has people in our life that want to destroy any faith that we begin to have in Jesus Christ; in other words, they want to sleep at night.

I believe most of you know the deal about Jesus Christ. God sent him to earth to right the ship and to teach people to truly care for one another. He performed miracles in front of thousands of people and became a threat to the political agenda of the times. He was sacrificed by God and murdered by the leaders of the world to save our souls. This was God's plan to offer us all the option of grace. He made Jesus Christ the gateway to Heaven. Simply put, God wants you to accept the key he is offering and open the door to Christ and, in return, Jesus will open the door to Heaven.

Getting to know Jesus Christ is not as difficult as you might think. I believe a good start would be getting a Bible and reading his words. Some Bibles have his quotes in red, and that will make it simple for you to see where he is coming from. After you get to know him a little, hit your knees and introduce yourself. Tell him that you would like to consider joining his team. Then ask if he could please forgive the sins that you have committed throughout your life. This will give you a fresh start, clean slate, and officially change your destination. Eternity, which is right around the corner, will somehow look much brighter for you! You will now be in possession of a special key!

DON'T LISTEN TO THE DEVIL

I was driving home from work after a nasty rainy day at the racetrack. My spirits were low and, in general, I was not very happy. Sammy, my dog, even put his paw on my arm, and that is always a pretty strong indication that things are not well. As I am driving, I passed this elderly man walking in the rain with an umbrella, a cane, and a small bag. My first thought was that he could be an Alzheimer's patient that was lost and walking in the rain. I thought that I should turn around and pick him up. The devil in my heart counters that thought with, "You had a bad day. Go home and eat lunch, and let someone else worry about him."

I keep driving. My next thought was, *He looked really old, and it is raining hard. Turn around and pick him up*!

The devil comes back with, "Cops drive down this road all the time. One will pick him up in a minute. Don't worry."

I keep driving. My next thought was, *The poor guy's wife might have thrown him out and, of all people, you can relate to that. Turn the truck around and go get him.*

Devil counters with, "You have Sam in the truck and not much room. He will be fine, and the rain is letting up anyway."

I keep driving and am now a couple of miles past the gentleman. My final thought was, *What if that was my father walking in the rain?*

As I am making my illegal U-turn, the devil takes one more desperate and final attempt, "The man might be an ax murderer, and you know the deal with picking up strangers."

My reply was, *I had a bad day and don't really care.*

I pull up to the possible ax murderer and roll down my window and ask him if he was okay. He said he was okay and was just walking back from a doctor's appointment to his boardinghouse. I asked him if he needed a lift, and he lit up like a Christmas tree! The boardinghouse was a few miles down the road. He was over seventy years old, and the devil was full of it. It was still raining hard. I moved some stuff around in the truck and had Sam jump in the back, and Joe joined me in the front seat. Joe was walking with a cane, an umbrella, and a bag. The devil, at this point, chimes back in to say that I should check the bag and that he told me so! I told him to go back to Hell!

Joe and I started talking, and he was in a lot of pain from something called neuropathy caused by diabetes. The pain was shooting down his leg, and he was not sure he could have made the walk. I told him that it was an honor to pick him up, and I felt that he was doing me a huge favor in accepting the ride. I told him about the horses and the track and gave him some passes for Monmouth Park. When Joe was getting out of the truck, he smiled, said he loved horses, and hoped to see me at the races. I hope to see him there as well.

While I was driving home, the day didn't seem that dreary anymore. Something had changed. I won a small battle that I really needed to win. Sammy even seemed to give me a look of approval. We all have battles like this every day, and it is very important which voice we listen to. Get it right, people. The little things mean a lot. Don't let the devil get you off course!

Ax murderer, really?

COMMANDMENTS MURDER

Repent: for the kingdom of Heaven is at hand.

—Jesus Christ

When reviewing the Ten Commandments, the one concerning murder shows up on the list. "You shall not murder." Pretty simple, right? You might think that this command would probably be the easiest one on the list to follow and obey. I would tend to agree, but there is a catch, and there might be millions of people caught in the net. Most people have a conscience that prevents them from murder. If your conscience doesn't save you, then the repercussions of committing murder might. The thought of spending the rest of your life in jail or the possibility of the electric chair could do the trick. Now let's say they change the rules and make it legal to kill people for any reason you choose. No repercussions, no reason to feel guilty. If you don't like someone and don't want them in your life, you can simply kill them! If society made it normal and acceptable to murder, then the murder rate in the world would increase dramatically. It would become popular and trendy to kill, and the headlines of the murders would include as many pictures that the press could get their hands on. The killers would become the heroes or the villains of the day, and the press would glamorize the good as well as the evil.

Okay, let's turn the page, so to speak, and talk about abortion. Abortion is legal in the United States and, in 2019, we had more than 625,000 reported abortions performed. The deaths of these babies were brought on for many reasons. I feel the majority of abortions performed are done so for convenience's sake. The couple are not married and certainly didn't plan or desire to have a child. The timing is off. The couple wants a child but not at this time. The pregnancy is brought on by a one-night stand, and following through with having a baby would be very inconvenient. Now we get to some truly difficult reasons to terminate a pregnancy. Let's say that a health check is done on your child in the womb, and things are not good. Your child is not only deformed but is going to be sick and in pain for his or her entire life. Let's say that you become pregnant due to rape and are left with that difficult decision. What to do if your husband abandons you and your two young children and you find out you are pregnant? You can't pay your current bills and are conflicted with adding another mouth to feed.

The sheer number of abortions in any given year shows that it has become acceptable in society and not considered murder to kill a child in the womb. The question you have to ask yourself is, does God consider it murder? Society is not going to judge you when you die, neither is the Supreme Court, the minister at your church, husband, family, or friends! God is going to be the Judge! I don't feel that it is wise to assume that you know how he is going to feel on any given issue, especially abortion. I can't see God being proabortion, but I am not here to judge. I am, however, going to tell you what you should do if you have had or supported an abortion.

Repentance is a gift from God for all of us! I can't tell you how many times throughout my life that I have sinned and was in need of forgiveness! Many times, I didn't even know I sinned, but through the grace of God, I know the importance of righting the ship and am not afraid to ask for help. When you repent, you ask God for forgiveness for a sin or lifestyle you have chosen and genuinely try to make amends. This should be followed up with a changing lifestyle and getting on the right path. I do not feel that repentance is a get-out-of-jail free card but must be done from the heart with pure intentions that are honorable and sincere. I believe, after repentance, a renewed relationship with God and Jesus Christ is in order. I feel it is critical that before we die, we all get our spiritual life in good standing. Repenting for a previous abortion or any sin, for that matter, is a very wise move, and it permanently clears that indiscretion from your soul. Once you repent, you are freed from the guilt of the sin, and a heavy burden is lifted forever.

Before I finish, I would like to bring men into the equation concerning abortion. I feel any man that has condoned an abortion, paid for an abortion, or in any way supported one is just as responsible as the pregnant mother. If God considers you an accomplice with this act, then your need for repentance should be front and center in your life. That old saying, "Do the right thing," comes to mind, and in this case, doing the right thing might be accepting responsibility for a tragedy, and asking God to forgive you.

Seeking peace with God is in all of our best interest! You have the right to choose the door of repentance and meet him halfway!

THE SIN, THE FALL, AND THE SPIRIT

Anyone who divorces his wife and marries another woman commits adultery, and the man who marries a divorced woman commits adultery.

—Jesus Christ

The following is a true story involving my personal journey. I believe it answers some interesting questions. The first being, does God try and correct us when we choose to sin? The second is, do family members that die keep an eye on us from Heaven?

Several years ago, after I was divorced the first time, I became friends with a gal that I had strong feelings for. I wasn't looking for a relationship, but the more time we spent together, the closer we became. Romance entered the equation, but there was a catch for me; she was still married. She had been separated from her husband for two years, but they never finalized the divorce. She explained that there were going to be financial complications, and she and her husband agreed to delay things for a while. For me, internally, I was having quite a struggle and tried to slow everything down. I knew that moving forward with the relationship was technically adultery. I also knew that adultery is a sin and punishable by a loving God! I kept going back and forth, looking for a way out of my paddock.

She was separated, right? That's kind of like divorced, right? She is a special gal, and I really feel strongly about her! I knew that I was walking a very fine line. The temptation was getting stronger every moment that we spent together and, finally, one night, we fell!

I remember waking up the next morning and going to work, and I actually felt very good. There wasn't a whole lot of guilt going on but memories of what I thought was a special night. God didn't share my definition of a special and came up with a plan to show me how much he loved me!

I train racehorses for a living, and one of my favorite things to do in the world was to ride my horse, Mountain. I had him since the day he was born, and he was my true soul mate. Even though he was very animated and cheeky at times, he always looked out for me. So the morning after my fall to sin, I put the saddle on Mountain, and off we went to the racetrack for a jog and gallop. We ended up making it about an eighth of a mile, and I sensed a change in Mountain. I wasn't sure what it was, but a few seconds later, I found out when he went crazy and started bucking! Mountain was a huge horse, and falling off him was like falling out of a building! I managed to stay on for a few seconds, but his final buck sent me flying. I landed awkwardly and felt a sharp pain in my right knee. Mountain calmly jogged down the track after he dislodged me like nothing ever happened and seemed quite happy with himself.

The outrider at the track came around to check on me and said he was going to send for the ambulance. I told him I was okay, but when I tried to get up, my knee buckled, and I went down again. My assistant from the barn arrived on the scene and helped me to get up and also helped me make it back to the barn.

Now comes the part about family members that died keeping an eye on you from Heaven. Two minutes after I hobbled back to the barn and got to my desk, the phone rang. I looked at the caller ID, and it's Karen, a close friend that was also very close to my mother who had passed a couple of years earlier. I felt it strange that Karen was calling at this time. It was very early in the morning, and I hadn't heard from her in a couple of months. She informed that she was driving to work on the New Jersey Turnpike and that my mother came to her in a very powerful way! She said she had to pull off the side of the road, and that's where she was calling me from. She explained that my mom communicated to her that she was very upset with me and wanted to ask, "What are you doing?"

Karen then asked if I knew what Mother was upset about. I admitted that I did and told her that we would discuss it another time. I then thanked her for passing on my mother's message. I feel this, without a doubt, proves that people do have souls and spirits that carry on after they die. I think my mother knew the dangers of the path I was on and wanted to pass on a warning. I also feel that she might have slapped Mountain on the butt right before he started bucking.

I found comfort in Karen's call and felt more strongly than ever that my mother was in Heaven. I also had a very strong sense of guilt and shame. I made a very poor decision when I knew better. I let the devil win at this game but was determined learn from my mistake. I went home, repented, and asked God to forgive me. I then called my partner in adultery and ended our relationship.

Let's talk about sin and the devil for a while. Make no mistake, Satan's methods are brilliant, and he is truly gifted concerning evil! He has turned family values and principles upside down and convinced the majority of people that sin is the new normal. He has everyone believing that God is kind and would never send a good person to Hell. I'm not so sure about that and feel many good people are not going to Heaven. They are not following God's plan involving Jesus Christ but taking a side road that the devil is offering! I honestly feel had I died when I fell off Mountain that morning that I earned a one-way ticket to Hell! There was going to be no debate and no escaping my destination.

I feel fortunate that I was given another opportunity to redeem myself through repentance. To be honest, I have probably needed a second chance a thousand over my lifetime. God has been very patient with me! I feel if you sin and are not forgiven, there is a good chance you are not going to Heaven! Make sure you take advantage of the gift of repentance and keep your eyes on eternity!

YOU SAVED ME

You shall love your neighbor as yourself.
—Jesus Christ

I was driving back to the barn to feed the horses this afternoon and had to take a detour due to construction. I pull up to a red light and stopped and noticed a man walking my way, pushing a grocery cart. The thought that everything he owned was in that cart crossed my mind. I rolled down my passenger window and said Hello. He was a little startled and surprised but responded with a smile and a Hello. He kept rolling his cart, and my light turned green, and we were going to part, never to see each other again. I quickly got a strong feeling that I should see if he needed help and turned the car around. When I pulled up to where he was, I asked him if he needed any help or any cash. My question seemed to bother him, and he seemed to wrestle with it for a while. He put his head in his hands and looked down. I got the sense that he was a proud man who was not comfortable asking for help. I encouraged him to come across the street to my window, and he finally did. I handed him some cash, and right away, he said, "Thank you!" He then very sincerely said, "You saved me."

I am not sure what caused us to cross paths, but I am very happy that we did. He made me realize how trivial the problems that I had been having were, and how fortunate and blessed I was. I ended up with tears of joy and the feeling that I really helped a man that needed a breath of fresh air. I hope my new friend finds his way home!

ASK AND YOU SHALL RECEIVE

I am the way and the truth and the life. No one comes to the Father except through me.

—Jesus Christ

To start this story, we are going to go back to when I was seven years old. Life was good. I had a mother and a father that loved me and a very caring older brother, and a baby sister on the way. We were living in a house in Aiken, South Carolina, and all was well. At this point in my life, I had a lot of faith in God. We used to get down on our knees at night and say prayers before bedtime, and I felt a great deal of comfort in knowing that God was there. Along comes a bump in the road. Mom and Dad started fighting, and after a very rough period, Dad left home. This changed everything and devastated our family, but I knew from what I had been taught about God that he could fix it! There was this 8-track tape that we had at the house by Glenn Campbell, and there was this song called "You Better Sit Down Kids." Some of the lyrics are:

> You better sit down kids, I've got something to
> say,
> Your mama is staying, but I'm going away.

I used to sit in the living room whenever I was alone and listened to that song over and over and cried and prayed to God to bring my daddy home. I probably did it for two years and after that came to the very strong conclusion that there was no God, or if there was, he sure didn't care about me!

Let's fast-forward twenty years. I have a very addictive personality, and if there was something you could get addicted to, you could sign me up. I had slain many of my demons, but the one that I couldn't beat were cigarettes. I had been smoking for nearly fifteen years and had a bad cough. I was also trying to be a good role model for my young son, so I tried very hard to quit. I went to a hypnotist, an acupuncturist, and then I went to some classes at a hospital in Red Bank, New Jersey. They had me walking around with a jar of nasty old cigarette butts and smell them each time I wanted a smoke. None of these things helped. I might have stopped for one day, but that was it. This was very frustrating for me, and I started feeling weak, depressed, and not much like a man.

One night, out of the blue, I decided to pray about it. I had not done much praying, since I felt God abandoned me but thought it might be my final option. Before I said my prayer, I sat on the bed and thought things through. I remembered hearing that in order to get to God, you had to go through his Son, Jesus Christ. There is a lot of history on Christ, and after thinking it through, it made a little sense to me. God sent his Son down to the earth to save the people! He healed the sick, raised the dead, and cast demons out of people's souls. He humbly taught people how to live in order to make it to Heaven and stay out of Hell.

After doing all this, his people abandoned him, hung him up on a cross, and killed him. With Jesus's dying breath, he asked God to forgive them. With all that being said, it made sense to me that Christ would hold the highest of positions! God put Jesus in charge of Heaven. If you want to meet God, see past loved ones, pets, and gain entrance to Heaven, you must reach out to Christ.

So after thinking this all through, I hit my knees at the foot of the bed and said a very simple prayer. I asked Jesus Christ, if he was there and was listening, could he please do me a favor and talk with God about my cigarette addiction? I told him that I had tried everything I could and was not even close. I told him that I was sick, frustrated, angry, and hopeless, and could he please do something to help? I talked with him just like I am talking with you guys right now. Like he was a friend, and I was simply asking for help. When I finished my prayer, I got up and crawled in bed and had thoughts of hope but also had thoughts of doubt. I must have had a sliver of faith and was soon to find out that Jesus put my prayer in front of God!

The next morning, I went to work at five and stopped by the store to get my pack of cigarettes and my cup of coffee. When I got to the counter, I did not ask the girl for the pack of smokes. It was kind of strange, but I headed to the barn without them. I do remember telling myself that I would be driving back to the store right after I had my coffee, which is a strong trigger to smoke. I had my coffee and had zero desire to smoke. Now God seriously had my attention! I didn't drive back to the store, and since that night I asked Jesus Christ for a little help, I have never had any desire to smoke another cigarette! God reached in and took the addiction right out of my body.

As you can imagine, this was a very powerful experience and opened the door to my faith that had been slammed shut so many years before! This led to a dramatic transformation in my life. Many other things have happened that have strengthened my faith, and I now know that the Father and Son are watching, and they want the best for all of us, and that includes you!

Before that night, when I prayed, I simply prayed to God and never addressed Jesus Christ. I didn't know about his teachings or God's command to communicate with his Son first, if you want to reach him. I can't stress enough the importance of including Jesus Christ in your prayers. He has done remarkable work for me, and I feel he will do the same for you.

DO YOU ALLOW THE DEVIL TO RAISE YOUR CHILDREN?

—Jesus Christ

I am hoping that after reading this story that unbelievers will consider exposing their children to the possibility of God, Jesus Christ, and faith.

I don't care which side of the fence you are on. You have to admit that quality of life, principles, and values are in sharp decline. Movies, TV, and the Internet seem darker than ever and focus on violence, sex, money, and poor character. The devil is pouring his energy into making the bad things in life seem normal and acceptable. He wants everyone of us to follow his lead and make poor decisions that will cost us dearly in the end! I don't believe Satan wants to do any of us any favors. He simply has a strong hatred for God! He knows that each and every one of us that he brings to Hell will deeply hurt the Lord, and he takes a great pride in that!

Whoever is reading this, you, your children, and families are hopefuls on the devil's list! He wins when he signs you up, and God, you, and your family will pay a deep price for his hatred! I honestly hope that even if you can't come to terms with a changing of faith that you at least expose and explain to your children that many people have a strong belief in God. Let them know that they shouldn't dismiss God simply because you do. Express that you will be pleased if they make their own decision over time. Let them know that you will be very supportive of them if they choose faith!

I know that all parents want the best for their children, so let's see if we can draw a few comparisons. Children that believe in God have a parent figure they can call on any time, night or day. Even when they don't feel comfortable speaking with you about a problem, having faith will allow them to speak with God without the fear of being judged. They also might receive some strong advice that will enable them to keep their head above water during difficult times. Raising children without God takes away this very important option when it might be needed the most! Being able to reach out to God adds a lot of confidence to your child, similar to them having a big brother always by their side.

This world can be a very lonely and unforgiving place! I went through some very rough patches when I was a young child. I spent a lot of time talking and praying to God. I personally am not sure I would still be here had it not been for my faith during those bad years. The big brother thing is huge, and I feel it's very dangerous for your son or daughter to be going through life alone and without God! You should also teach your kids to respect and fear the devil, just like you would teach them to be very afraid of a rattlesnake!

I have spent time studying the Bible and near-death experiences, and one of the common denominators is that the people that are in Hell have a very strong desire to warn the living not to go there! They want to share how brutal it is and convince anyone that will listen to take steps to go to Heaven! There is a story in the Bible about a rich man that was sent to Hell. His main desire was to have a spirit from the dead go and warn his five brothers so they would repent and escape Hell! His request was denied, but you have to wonder how he would have felt if he knew that his son or daughter were soon going to join him in Hell. I honestly can't imagine a worse feeling for a parent to have!

So that's what I have for you. I hope you clearly understand that I want the absolute best for you and your family! I hope you consider what I have written and fight to look out for your children! I also hope you yourself consider changing teams and keeping the family intact! You don't want to go there.

DO ANGELS COME TO VISIT?

—Jesus Christ

When I am training racehorses in Aiken, I have one steady rider and hire freelance riders when I need the two-year-olds to go out in pairs. The freelance riders show up very early in the morning before they go to work for their own outfits, and we get the babies out in the dark. A couple of weeks ago, I had the riders come in on Sunday so we could take the babies up to the main track and school them in the gate. I don't like training on Sunday and believe in following God's advice, or shall we say commandment, and have a day of rest! I rationalized a bit and trained anyway. This week, I was going to do the same but, for some reason, I was struggling with it. I am not only working on Sunday myself but also asking other people to do it as well.

Friday, I was in the acute care psychiatric ward in Charleston, South Carolina. I am sorry to disappoint many of my "close friends," but I was not being committed! I was there to visit a friend. I was waiting to talk with my friend, and a tall man with long red hair approached me on the couch. He introduced himself and said he was a patient in the hospital. He seemed very kind and coherent and had my attention. There was something about him that I liked. He indicated that he was in the hospital because of his faith, and then he hit me with a question that had me scratching my head! He asked me if I knew that "working on the Sabbath is a sin"? He explained that it is one of the commandments and should be taken more seriously!

This was sort of a "wow moment" because I was thinking about it a lot on the way to Charleston. I looked at him with a smile on my face and came up with my best defense. I explained to him that I worked with horses, and they require care seven days a week. I then mentioned that Christ even used a sheep as an excuse to work on the Sabbath. He was much better versed with the Bible than I, and we sat and talked for a while. I really enjoyed our conversation, and when I went back to work on Saturday morning, I cancelled our Sunday training session!

So the question remains, does God send angels when we are struggling for answers? Or was my new friend at that hospital at the time with that specific advice just by coincidence? I am going with angels in the psych ward in Charleston, South Carolina, and they might be putting me in there next week to join my friend!

THE PRODIGAL SON

Judge not, and you shall not be judged:
condemn not, and you shall not be condemned:
forgive and you shall be forgiven.

—Jesus Christ

There is a story in the Bible about the prodigal son. Looking up the word *prodigal*, you will find the following: "Spending money or resources freely and recklessly; wastefully extravagant." So Jesus Christ tells this story, and I feel his intentions were to describe the importance of rescuing our soul from sin, and the celebration in Heaven for each and every one of us that is saved.

So as the story goes, a certain man had two sons. The younger son asked his father to give him his inheritance early. The father granted his wish, and the young man packed his belongings and traveled to a faraway country. He then proceeded to waste all that he had with riotous living. He ended up dead broke and surviving on food that was meant for pigs. The many friends that he had disappeared as soon as the riches ran out. This very humbling experience brought him to the conclusion that he should go back home to his father and ask if he could work as a hired hand.

His father saw him walking from a distance, and joy filled his heart! He ran to his son and hugged and kissed him. The father ordered his servants to bring his son new clothes, a ring to put on his hand, and sandals for his feet. He then ordered up a special party for his son's return and spared no expense. This celebration was a very happy event for everyone, except for the older brother. He couldn't come to terms with his younger brother running off, living with harlots, and wasting his father's money. To be honest, I might have had a difficult time with this as well and needed to listen to Jesus's point. Christ explained, and here is the father's explanation to the older brother in Jesus's words, "Son, thou art ever with me, and all that I have is thine. It was meet that we should make merry, and be glad: for this thy brother was dead, and is alive again; and was lost, and is found."

I hope each and every one of you realize the point that Jesus Christ was driving home. If you are a sinner, come home to him, and he will forgive and welcome you into his family. There will be big celebration in Heaven just for you, and God will be smiling as he writes you down as one of his own! Luke 15:7 explains this well: "Just so, I tell you, there will be more joy in Heaven over one sinner who repents than over 99 righteous persons who need no repentance." Let's bring a lot of joy to Heaven, people! Get to know God and Jesus Christ and come home!

One more thing I want to share with you is that Christ spoke to unbelievers in parables. A good description of a parable is that it is an earthly story with a Heavenly meaning. Jesus explains why he spoke in parables in Matthew 13:11. He said, "Because it is given onto you to know the mysteries of the kingdom of Heaven but to them it is not given." So what Jesus was saying here is that some things are hidden from a lot of people. He is trying to offer unbelievers understanding through his stories. He then wants to save you if you can muster up some faith in him and repent of your sins. You might be one of those people that is blocked from knowing the truth by the devil. I hope you can overcome being blocked with blind faith in the Father, Son, and Holy Spirit! They will be throwing you an amazing party in Heaven!

HORSES SENDING
MESSAGE

*But the Advocate, the Holy Spirit, whom the Father
will send in my name, will teach you all things and
will remind you of everything I have said to you.*

—Jesus Christ

Several years ago, I had something interesting happen with a horse of mine named Catechol. I got home from the barn one day, ate lunch, and settled in on the couch. I closed my eyes and was just about to fall asleep when Catechol's face appeared like a dream. As soon as it did, I had an extremely sharp pain in my right foot that made me nearly jump off the couch! I didn't really understand what happened and, after several minutes, I started to settle back in again. As soon as I relaxed and shut my eyes again, we had round two. Catechol's face followed by a more intense pain in my right foot! This time, it got my full attention, and I called my assistant at the barn and asked him to go down and check on Catechol from head to toe. I stayed on the phone with him while he was checking, and the report came back that his right foot was very hot, and he was lame on it walking around the stall. I headed back to the barn to see what was going on. He had been shod the day before, and after looking him over, I felt the inside heel nail might have been a little high. We pulled it out, tubbed him, and packed his feet. The following morning, he was fine!

Over the years, this has happened many other times with my knee or ankle, and it has always held true. Yesterday, when I was driving down to Aiken, South Carolina, I started getting another stabbing pain in my right foot. I tried to ignore it and thought it was from driving. But the more I ignored it, the worse it got! I finally got the message and called my assistant again. I explained what was happening and told him to go down the line and check every horse's feet! I heard laughter on the other end, and he explained that it wasn't a horse but my rider's foot that was hurt! Right about the time my foot started hurting, Fox Tree bucked my rider off in the shed row and hurt his right foot! As soon as I got off the phone, the pain stopped. Once the message was received, no longer was there a need to keep sending. The Holy Spirit is alive and well in me. I am a little curious about what would happen to me if one of my friends was shot.

DEFINITION OF A
TRUE MIRACLE

Take heed that ye despise not one of these little ones; for
I say unto you, That in Heaven their angels do always
behold the face of my Father which is in Heaven.

—Jesus Christ

Thirty years ago, my son, Parker, and I were invited to go tubing by a friend that had a boat on the Navesink River in New Jersey. Tubing is when you tie a large inner tube to a rope, and someone rides the tube while it's being pulled by a boat. Generally, the idea is for the person to ride for a while, and then the driver of the boat tries to get them off by making sharp turns and having the tube jump the wakes. This day was no exception, and my friend, Bernie, did not disappoint. I decided to go first to show my son, Parker, who was about ten at the time, how it was done. I dove in the water, swam back to the tube, and climbed onboard. Bernie started out slow, and I was having a blast, and then he started picking up his game a bit. He was ducking and diving, and I was holding on for all I was worth. I ended up hitting this big wake and was sent airborne. I crashed with a big splash, and everyone in the boat was cracking up.

Parker insisted that it was his turn, and I knew that he was going to have a blast, so off he went. He climbed on the tube, and Bernie was kind to him for a few minutes but soon realized that Parker was very athletic and like a cat on the tube. Bernie started picking up speed and making turns to no avail, Parker was not coming off! This went on for a few more minutes, and this is where things started to get a little strange. Bernie hits the gas and then makes this very sharp turn. I am in the back of the boat, watching Parker and encouraging him to hang on but also playing the traitor by telling Bernie to get him off! When Bernie made the sharp turn, a lot of slack came in the rope, and the tube jumped forward. All people that ride horses for any length of time fall off and know the feeling that I am about to describe. Everything slows way down. While you are in the air and falling, it seems to be in slow motion for some reason.

When Parker's tube jumped forward, things slowed way down for me. I watched in horror as the nylon rope looped around my son's neck. I knew at the speed we were traveling, he was going to be dead in a matter of seconds. The rope was going to break his neck. I screamed, and my legs buckled, and I fell to my knees in the boat. It was at this moment that I witnessed an undeniable miracle and came to the definite conclusion that we do have angels that look over us. The nylon rope that was a few inches thick and could tow a truck, broke before the slack came out! It broke in midair, a split second before it was going to kill Parker!

At this point, I collapsed and sat in the back of the boat with tears in my eyes. Bernie did not know what happened, and Parker didn't even know. They were both wondering how the rope could have broken and why I couldn't talk for a couple of minutes. I had this overwhelming sense of joy and relief that I was dealing with. I knew why the rope broke. I knew that I had just been blessed by a very special angel and that my son's life had just been spared.

It is my opinion that there are miracles, and we do have angels. God, Jesus Christ, and the Holy Spirit are here for you. You simply have to open the line of communication, and you might be amazed with what you discover! They are waiting for you just like they were waiting for me. Reach out and give faith a chance.

SOME ANSWERS
FOR ADDICTION

"And lead us not into temptation, but deliver us from evil."
—Jesus Christ

Addiction has recently become front and center in the news. It has also been one of my greatest challenges throughout my life. I am truly an expert when it comes to addiction! I am writing this post in hopes that I might help prevent some people from getting addicted or help them weather the storm if they have already taken the turn down that road. They say that addiction is a disease, and that it runs in the family. I strongly agree that it is genetic, and it definitely runs in the family.

Warning #1: If you have family members before you that have battled with addiction, whether it be alcohol, drugs, gambling, or others, you need to be acutely aware that you are much more suscep-tible to facing the same problem. I want to be clear; I am not blaming my addiction on my genes or family. There are millions of people that have this in their family that have not become addicted to any-thing. I claim full responsibility for my past. When I look back, one of the things that I remember is that my tolerance for alcohol and drugs went through the roof very quickly. Normal people would go out to a bar and have one or two drinks and were happy with the feeling and leave it at that. I started out that way but very quickly needed seven or eight drinks to achieve the same feeling. The same went for narcotic painkillers. I have had several physical issues over the years and had surgery on my knees and back. When I started to take painkillers, my tolerance also went up very quickly. I started out taking one pill every four hours but very quickly went up to three pills every two or three hours.

Warning #2: If you notice your tolerance to alcohol or drugs rising quickly, I feel it is a strong signal that you are in the beginning stages of addiction, and you should seriously consider walking away from those substances and staying away!

My drug of choice was painkillers. Percocet and Vicodin were my favorites. These types of medications are the main problem that is currently sweeping our country and leading to the accidental overdoses and deaths from heroin and fentanyl. When I take painkillers, not only does it kill any pain I am having, but it also tweaks my brain and gives me a very euphoric feeling. I have spoken with a lot of people about this and feel that normal people get tired when they take these types of meds, but not the addict. It wakes our mind up and makes us feel very alert and alive.

Warning #3: If you consume any drugs or alcohol that make you feel euphoric, confident, or happier than you are normally are, stay as far away as possible, because it won't be long before you want and need that feeling all the time!

Why are people dying from heroin and fentanyl? I checked into a drug and alcohol rehab in Charleston, South Carolina, called Chaps Baker. I did this about thirty years ago and honestly believe it saved my life. Back then and up until just recently, the narcotics were easily obtained. I maintained a twenty-pill-a-day habit for years. The addict can get very clever when it comes to getting his meds with the thought of running out and the agony of withdrawal right around the corner. I will tell you an entertaining story about a trip to the ER. Every once in a while, I would be on the verge of running out of pills and have to go to the emergency room. Like I said before, I had lots of problems with my back, and it was easy for me to convince a doctor that I needed drugs. It was one of those half-truth sort of things.

So when I get in the room, and the doctor shows up, he brings with him eight med students. From my previous surgeries and dealing with all the doctors, I knew what to say and when to cringe. I went through my routine, and all the students were attentively observing as the doctor went through his. When he completed his examination, he asked the students for their opinion. Happily, from my perspective, they all recommended some form of painkiller along with some physical therapy. Then something strange happened. The doctor asked all of the students to leave the room. As soon as they left, Doc put this big smile on his face, looked me right in the eye, and said, "You are here to get painkillers, aren't you?"

I couldn't help it and busted out laughing, and then he started laughing as well. I asked him how he knew and told him that I thought my performance was masterful in front of the students. He said he had a gut feeling and needed to see if he was right. He asked me if I would do him a big favor and open up to his students and tell them the truth. I happily agreed and sat with his students for a half an hour, teaching addiction 101. I actually really enjoyed it and felt it was an eye-opener for the students. The doctor thanked me very much, shook my hand, and urged me to get help with my addiction. I took him up on his advice and checked into Chaps Baker later that year. Sorry about the sidetrack, and we are going to get back to work.

Withdrawal is a horrible feeling. It not only devastates you physically but also mentally as well. You are not capable of going through normal daily activities when you are in withdrawal. It feels like having the flu, only ten times worse, and it lasts for about a week. It puts you in a state of depression, fear, and desperation that I promise you never want to experience! I feel the reason for all the heroin and fentanyl deaths is that people are now finding it impossible to obtain the prescription drugs, and their only way of preventing withdrawal is to turn to the street drugs. They are buying heroin from some very shady characters and honestly have no clue what they are getting. This is one of those Catch-22 deals; the pharmaceutical and medical professions are trying to right the ship with the painkillers, but doing so is leading to the deaths of many addicts. I am not sure what the answer is, but I hope we find some middle ground until we get a better handle on this!

Warning #4: Do not ever buy something off the streets and put it in your veins! Stay with a friend, check into rehab, do what you have to do to avoid that situation! The withdrawal will ease in a few days, and you will feel better! Drink tons of water to speed the recovery!

My final *warning*: Don't ever be afraid or feel ashamed to get help with any type of addiction. There are two kinds of help. The help that I received in rehab was priceless, and I'm pretty sure that I wouldn't still be here if I hadn't taken that step. The other type of help is through prayer.

If you have a problem that you don't feel you can handle, pray to Jesus Christ and ask him to speak with God on your behalf. I have a feeling that you might really be surprised with the results.

DEVIL CHILDREN

The field is the world; the good seed are the children of the kingdom; but the tares are the children of the wicked one.

—Jesus Christ

I feel one of the most important things that any good person or Christian can learn is how to spot a child of the devil. There are millions of them out there, and their intentions are in total opposition to yours. Christians are very willing to share their faith and have a genuine desire to help others. They are even willing to help and pray for the children of Satan. The devil, on the other hand, does not allow his family to reveal themselves or their true intentions. He keeps them in the dark so they can fulfill his duties.

Let's focus on the devil's own that know who their daddy is and are very loyal to his cause! I feel the devil is personally close to certain people, and they share his dreams. These individuals have very dark souls but are gifted at hiding their intentions behind a charming smile. The devil sends this group after people that follow God, Jesus Christ and other people who are yet undecided where they stand; in other words, people that are a threat to his kingdom, their job here on earth is to infiltrate certain people's lives and throw them off course by any means possible. Trust me, they are very good at their craft! These individuals could come in the form of a friend, coworker, parent, child, or even your spouse. The closer they are to you, the more vulnerable you are to their schemes. The pain and disappointment they inflict runs deep, and they use your loyalty, integrity, and feelings against you in a battle for your soul. When I quote the Bible, I prefer to quote the sayings of Christ. And in Matthew 10:36, Jesus said, "And a man's foes shall be those of his own household." He follows that up with letting people know that if it comes between choosing faith or family, always choose faith!

So how do we spot these rascals? One of the most simple ways is to ask them about their faith in God and Jesus Christ. They might be able to claim some faith in God but, trust me, it won't be your God. It will be the god of this world, Lucifer. They will never be able to claim faith and loyalty to Jesus Christ, and that is critical in figuring out whose team they play for! Devil children might try and ease your concerns by telling you they are working on having faith in Christ and feel like they are close. You should counter that with an offer to study the Bible with them and read some of Jesus's sayings. My prediction is things won't go well, and that will give you a clue of who you are dealing with.

Another possible way to figure out someone's faith-line would be to ask them to financially or publicly back a Christian cause. They will have a very difficult time doing this and will ultimately find a way to bow out. You can equate them helping Jesus with someone asking you to back a very evil cause; something dark, destructive, and vile that goes against every principle in your body! You wouldn't be able to do it, and I feel it will be next to impossible for them to support Christ on any level! I can't stress enough how dangerous these individuals are! You should make it a lifetime priority to distance yourself from the destruction that they will try and bring into your life. Let me try and give you a couple more examples of how to spot the dark souls. Let's say you are a good person or a Christian and make the mistake of getting into a relationship with a devil's advocate. They will never be able to build you up and lead you to having more confidence in yourself or your faith. You will always be left wanting. You could have a great accomplishment at work, and when it is revealed, it will be brushed off. Even if it benefits them a great deal to be supportive and encouraging, it won't happen! You will be left wondering why. But if you truly evaluate your relationship from the beginning, you will realize that they never were sincerely behind you!

Another possible way to do a soul check is to invite your honey to meet one of your close Christian friends. They will have a very difficult time sitting through dinner without revealing their dislike and possible hatred for your friend. This would compare with them taking you to dinner with one of their friends who is a dark and shady individual. You probably wouldn't be able to hide your feelings for very long, and neither will they!

Let's say that that you make a tragic error in judgement and are engaged to a devil child. God will provide a way out! There will be a moment in time that it becomes crystal clear that you do not want to spend the rest of your life with this individual! This might happen a couple of months before your wedding or it might happen the day before. I highly recommend that you listen to your instincts, aka Holy Spirit, who is screaming NO! You might think that you have already made the plans, and it will be a disappointment to your family, friends, and your fiancé, but trust me, one day of disappointment is far better than a match made in Hell.

I want to be clear; there are millions of children of the devil and also millions of men and women who are undecided in their faith. Just because someone has not found God or Christ does not make them a bad person or a devil's advocate. You need to use your own discernment to figure that out. I have simply given you some options to use to help you along the way. Don't be fooled by the evil ones!

One more thing I want to add before I go is, don't be surprised when you are working on a project for God or something special that the devil will send distracters! Someone will call with upsetting news or out of the blue need help from you with a project. The timing of their contact could be a clear warning! Several times while writing this book, I have gotten calls from "loved ones" that have been a clear attempt to throw me off. When this happens to you, and you realize what's going on, politely shut them down and finish what's important to you and then address their situation later. Hopefully, I have given you some things to consider when dealing with the devil's own. They do not have good intentions or your best interest at heart. Keep your distance at all costs!

KNOWING OF
DEATH BRINGS ONE
CLARITY IN LIFE

Today shalt thou be with me in paradise.

—Jesus Christ

My mother developed liver cancer and was given months to live. The following are lessons that we both learned on this journey.

One of the first things I want to share I am not proud of, but it is relevant to the story. When Mom got sick, I took some time off from work, brought my horse, Mountain, down to Aiken, South Carolina, and spent several months with her. During this time together, I often reflected on how well she was handling the death sentence given to her by her doctors. I was very proud of her and amazed with her courage! I wondered how I would deal with similar news. I felt, in my mind, that I would deal with it very well but was soon to be taught that I was not as strong and brave as I thought I was!

One day, Mom and I were both having a bad day. She was scared and showing weakness that I was not accustomed to seeing. She felt understandably sorry for herself, but my internal reaction was not one of understanding. In my mind, I was thinking that she had led a blessed life and was fortunate. I also felt like she should handle this like I would if I were in a similar situation, with her shoulders back and looking forward to going to Heaven and seeing old friends and family that she loved! I don't believe that God was pleased with my thoughts and decided to send me to dying school!

I was getting ready for bed that night and, all of a sudden, I had a sharp pain in my side. This was in the same place that Mom used to

48

reach for when she was hurting. The pain only lasted a few seconds, but it definitely got my attention! I was a little scared and was trying to figure out what happened when, all of a sudden, round two comes! Same place on my side, only much more intense, and drops me to the floor! Now I'm on the ground with tears of pain in my eyes, and a thought is placed in my head. I have the same cancer that my mom has, and I am going to die! I'm not sure how to explain this, but the thought wasn't mine, but it was clear and definite that I was soon to die!

As I lay there on the ground, my shoulders weren't back. I was not looking forward to going to Heaven and had no desire to see any deceased relatives! I had a powerful sense of fear and worse was a feeling of loneliness that was heart-wrenching! So much for bravery.

This event lasted about five minutes, and then the pain and knowledge of my imminent death disappeared as quickly as it came. I climbed in bed and sat there and thought things through. I was being taught a lesson concerning pride and compassion and to this day feel it was a gift from God. I will tell you this, I have an enormous amount of respect for people who know they are going to die and live well until the end.

I'm going to end with a night that Mom and I spent sitting on her bed. She went to the bank and brought home all the contents of her safety deposit box. She had a lot of very beautiful jewelry, and we were dividing things up to be given to my sister, brother, and myself. This was a very heartfelt evening, and she decided to show me what dying was teaching her. Throughout her life, she loved beautiful and expensive things. Her clothes, her jewelry, her cars were all top of the line and meant the world to her! So while we were sitting there and she had about thirty days to live, she began to explain that all of her material possessions meant nothing to her now! She demonstrated regret for all the attention she gave them in the past. She started talking about how much her relationships with her family, friends, pets, God, and Jesus Christ meant to her now! She told me that these should be the main focus in my life and not worldly possessions.

We spent the last month of her life having visits with family and friends, spending time with my horse, Mountain, and her dogs,

Dicky and Bo Bo. We also read the Bible every night. Her favorite verse was Psalm 23, and it goes like this:

> The Lord is my shepherd; I shall not want.
> He maketh me to lie down in green pastures: he leadeth me beside the still waters.
> He restoreth my soul: he leadeth me in the paths of righteousness for his name's sake.
> Yea, though I walk through the valley of the shadow of death, I will fear no evil: for thou art with me; thy rod and thy staff they comfort me.
> Though preparest a table before me in the presence of mine enemies: thou anointest my head with oil; my cup runneth over.
> Surely goodness and mercy shall follow me all the days of my life: and I will dwell in the house of the Lord forever.

That last part about dwelling in the house of the Lord forever is key! My mother is there now, and I hope to see her again in the future! I hope that everyone reading this chooses to join us!

BRING SOMETHING TO HEAVEN WHEN YOU GO

Follow me and I will make you fishers of men.
—Jesus Christ

Someone asked me last week if I had a strong desire to win the Kentucky Derby. I thought about it for a moment, and my mind and I said no. This had me scratching my head, and I asked myself the question again. This time, I felt a little sad and came back with a more resolute no. I have been training racehorses for over forty years. The derby is probably every trainer's dream race to win in America, but for me, right now, that burning desire is gone. It has been replaced with the desire to do a good job with this book and save a few souls along the way. I still love working with the horses and have two mares in training now. Their names are Power and Glory and Judgement Time. I really enjoy getting up early in the morning and spending a few hours outside, working with them. I took some time off after the Monmouth Park season last year and, to be honest, I felt lost and empty. The horses are like air for me, and I feel it is in my best interest to stay in touch with them. Training two horses is perfect and allows me to focus on my new calling.

I started writing this book about seven years ago and kept putting it off to follow the racing world. God was patient with me, but the patience ran out last year, and he made it clear I needed to get back to work for him. I was humbled and thankful for his direction, and here we are today. Just like me, I feel most people put the majority of their energy and focus into the here and now. Heaven and Hell are an afterthought and rarely come to mind unless there is an

52

accident or illness. People don't think about what they are going to say to God when he asks, "What did you do for my kingdom and my people?" I personally would not have had a good answer for him last year, but I'm working on that.

They say that when you die, you can't bring anything with you to Heaven. That's not true. You can! You can bring men, women, and children to Heaven! I could spend the rest of my days on earth trying to win the derby but feel it would be a shallow accomplishment compared meeting people in Heaven that are there because I helped them with a strengthening of their faith! Now that would be a special celebration for all of us; walking through the gates of Heaven and meeting many souls that we helped find their way. I hope everyone reading this realizes that we do go somewhere when we die, and that it is vital that we get our spiritual house in order! Get in touch with God and Jesus Christ and start making a difference for them here on earth. Do some things that will make you proud to walk before the Lord when that day comes.

HOLY POST OFFICE

For whosoever shall be ashamed of me and of my words, of him shall the Son of man be ashamed.

—Jesus Christ

I have to say that I am in shock! I went in the post office to mail a friend's Christmas present today. While I was there, I actually heard the word *God*! I have not heard this word out in public much lately, as it is apparently very offensive and seems to upset a lot of people. The G-word now appears to be more offensive for Americans than the f-word and has been banned from many public places. As I was standing in line, I was observing a man going through the routine of getting his passport. He was filling out paperwork and answering questions from a gal that worked at the post office. Then it suddenly happened. She asked him to raise his right hand and swear to God that he was telling the truth about the questions! My jaw dropped, I dropped my friends present, and put my hands to my head! I honestly couldn't believe it. How could the atheist miss the post office? Are you kidding me!

Another guy in the line was shocked as well, and we both looked at each other and said, "Did we just hear that right?" The dude that proudly took the oath was walking by, and I had to stop him. I asked, "Did they just ask you to swear to God?"

He smiled and said, "Yes," they did, and he couldn't believe it either!

As he walked by, I patted him on the shoulder, and said, "I hope you told the truth."

We both started laughing, and this all brought a very big smile to my face. When I finished mailing my friend's gift and was walking out, a thought came to mind. *For years, we haven't had any postal workers go postal.* I thought about this for a few seconds and came to the conclusion that the post office is one of the only places left that God can hang out!

THE HOLY SPIRIT

And I will ask the Father, and he will give you another
advocate to help you and be with you forever.

—Jesus Christ

I came back to the barn this afternoon to feed and care for my horses. When I was finished, I took the dogs for a walk around the polo field. As I was loading the dogs in the car to head home, I heard a loud bang in a neighboring barn. I initially thought a horse kicked the wall but listened just in case a horse was cast or stuck up against the wall. When a horse gets stuck, you will hear the initial loud noise, and it will be followed up by a lot more noise. After a couple of minutes of hearing nothing more, I assumed that all was well. In my mind, I was cleared to go home. When I started up the car, something inside of me issued a warning. I had a strong feeling that I was not good to go and that I should make sure everything was okay.

This feeling could be attributed to a gut feeling or I could go biblical and say it was the Holy Spirit. I do not feel my gut is that smart or knew that a horse was in serious danger, so I'm going biblical! Jesus Christ defined the Holy Spirit in the Bible as a spiritual helper that is sent by God. I believe this to be true and can't count how many times over my lifetime that my Helper has guided me in the right direction.

So now I am sitting in the car, having this debate in my head as to whether I should walk over to the barn or not. Logic says I don't need to and that a horse simply kicked the wall. The Holy Spirit is not into logic and directed me to get my lazy butt out of the car and go check! When I got to the barn, I immediately saw a very dangerous situation! I was correct about the kick but did not know that when this filly kicked, that her foot went through the back door of her stall and was hopelessly stuck. I initially felt I could pull the bottom of the door open enough so the filly could slide her foot out. She must have kicked it with a lot of force because I pulled it as hard as I could, and it wouldn't budge! Plan B was to open the door, but I quickly realized that was going to be a challenge. The people in charge of the barn installed screws in the latches to prevent horses from opening the back door! Now I was really scared! I didn't have a screwdriver and wasn't sure how much longer this beautiful filly was going to handle the situation.

At this point, I started praying, and I promised the filly that I was going to find a way to get her out! I ran back over to my barn and found a solid piece of board that I thought might be able to knock the screws out of the latch. After several attempts, I finally got it done and was able to open the door. The filly was amazingly classy and smart while all this was going on, and I believe she also had a spirit that was keeping her calm. I was making a lot of noise when hitting the screws and, had she panicked, she would have broken her leg. I walked around, petted her on the head, and said a prayer to God, Jesus Christ, and my Holy Spirit. I thanked them for having me there at that time and insisting that I go check on the noise. I asked them to make sure that the filly was going to be okay and then called the trainer of the filly and explained what happened. All is well.

LUCIFER

—Jesus Christ

The story goes that Lucifer is a fallen angel. He was once very close to God, but as will happen in close working relationships, sooner or later, the assistant comes to the conclusion that he knows much more than the boss and wants to take over the position. It sounds like Lucifer's power and ego got the better of him, and he made the ultimate mistake; he lashed out at God. This was not a wise choice and probably led to the creation of Hell and Lucifer's fall from grace. I feel his fall has fueled his anger, and he is now doing his best to have as many of God's children as possible join him in Hell. The problem is, he is very good at what he does!

There is discussion in the Bible about forgiveness. It is very clear that in order to be forgiven for your sins, you must be willing to forgive other people that have sinned against you. Not only is it healthy for you to forgive, but also it might very well be a requirement to make it into Heaven. I can find no mention anywhere in the Bible about forgiving the devil. When Jesus Christ was hanging on the cross and taking his last breaths, he asked God to forgive the people that crucified him, yet you do not see Christ demonstrating any mercy for Lucifer. This does have me a little confused, but I feel the devil turned very vile and evil and has caused unimaginable suffering here on earth and in Hell. He has passed any road to redemption and is choosing to remain God's adversary. This choice makes you

61

his enemy and, trust me, he is very good at getting people to sign up for his team.

Now we get to the interesting part. Christ, on more than one occasion, mentioned that there are children of God and children of the devil. He said that your enemy might very well be sitting across the table from you at dinner. In other words, your father, mother, brother, sister, husband, wife, or children might be playing for the other team. I feel close friends can also fall into this group. I think some people come into your lives to trip you up and try and cause confusion, pain, and suffering. The older I get, the easier these critters are to spot, and I no longer care to spend much time with them!

The question I have is, do these people know that they are children of the devil, and do they take pride in their work? I feel that, hopefully, I am one of God's children and feel like I have a good heart. I mess up from time to time but, for the most part, I try and do the right thing and have good intentions. I am very proud to try and serve the Father, Son, and Holy Spirit and hope I can make a difference and save a few souls along the way.

The question remains, are the evil people doing their job with intent and knowledge or is it simply their nature and "they know not what they do?" I honestly hope they don't know and can't help themselves. This will make dinner a little more pleasant on certain occasions.

Okay, let's get back to Lucifer. As I said, he is brilliant at what he does! He plays a much better game than his Christian counterparts. He uses his resources in the best possible way to bring as many people to Hell as he can, and he is very successful! A lot of religious organizations do very good things in other countries. They spend a lot of resources digging wells and teaching people how to plant food and live a better life. This is all well and good, but the devil has used his time and resources in Hollywood and on social media and has thrown out a wide net that is constantly full.

The world is getting darker by the day, and Christians are getting left behind and doing little to stop it! I honestly don't feel great about our immediate future and feel everyone should get their house in order. I am praying that we turn some things around and give God a glimmer of hope. He deserves better from all of us! I wouldn't be doing my job if I didn't try and convince people that Hell might not be their best landing spot!

I feel Christians know the watered-down version of gaining entry into Heaven. The preachers have made it simplistic and easy in order to keep their flock happy and keep the numbers up. I feel the opposite is true and entry to Heaven is a lot more complex and difficult than everyone is being taught! I think a lot of people believe once they accept Christ and repent, that they are good to go and saved for life. Nice thought, but I wouldn't count on it! Christ healed a man that had been sick for thirty-eight years, and after he did, he gave the man a warning: "Behold, thou art made whole: sin no more, lest a worse thing come unto thee." I feel this clears up the thought that "once saved always saved" and that people should very much be on guard how they conduct their lives until the day they take their last breath! I feel that Heaven has a purity level that cannot be altered and that any sin, even if it is a small one that is still on your books, stops you in your tracks from entering Heaven!

The bad news is that once you are stopped at the gates of Heaven, you are sent to Hell. I know this sounds very harsh, and I don't like it either, but I don't get to make up the rules. I feel Jesus did try and help with the Lord's Prayer. The prayer asks for repentance and protection from evil. I feel it would probably be a very good prayer to say every morning before you start your day!

Now let's take a shot at the people that play for the other team, or as Christ called them, children of the evil one. Like I said, I do not know if you know you play for the devil or if you just have this sense of darkness about you that you don't understand. I do know one thing, and that is that your leader, the devil, is not the one in charge! Backing, trusting, or following him is very foolish and going to ensure your one-way ticket to the misery of Hell. The question you have to ask yourself is what happens when you get to Hell and what is it like down there? It sounds like there will be only two options for you in Hell. You will either be torturing other souls or you will be tortured yourself. I wouldn't count on any loyalty from Lucifer. He betrayed God, and he won't blink an eye before betraying you!

Fortunately, you have one more option, but the offer is only good while you are still breathing! You have the opportunity to change teams! Please don't take this offer lightly! God gave up his Son, and Christ gave up his life in order to seal this deal. This sacrifice was unimaginable and should be met with the utmost respect and gratitude! I feel changing teams was also made very easy for you. You don't need to shout from the rooftops that you are now a Christian! You don't need to tell anyone; you can keep it between you and Christ! I lost my faith when I was an eight-year-old boy when several tragedies hit my family. I got it back fifteen years later when I asked Jesus Christ in a simple prayer if he was there and, if so, could he please help me? He answered my prayer in dramatic fashion and let me know that he and God were real and were there for me.

I have a feeling if you say a simple prayer and ask Christ for forgiveness and welcome him into your life, you might be pleasantly surprised with the results! Like I said, this does not need to be a public announcement. You can go in your closet, shut the door, and say this prayer. Let him know that you are a free agent and want to change teams! Repent and apologize for your sins and try and move in the direction of the Father and Son! This will hopefully lead to your victory over the devil and a glorious journey to Heaven!

TEMPTATION

*Watch and pray, that you enter not into temptation:
the spirit indeed is willing, but the flesh is weak.*

—Jesus Christ

Temptation comes in many forms, and for two New Jersey based horse trainers, it showed up on their doorstep as illegal undetectable drugs for their horses. These drugs would enable Jason and Jorge to win races at a remarkable clip! They were not only raking in a lot of money but were also enjoying that amazing feeling of winning race after race and defeating their peers on a regular basis. Jason and Jorge were competing at the highest level, and this brought fame into the picture. You can't get enough of fame; it's addictive! So how did they get there? I feel some clever individuals probably approached the trainers and simply told them that they came up with a medication that would greatly improve the quality of their horses! They might have promoted the drug as not only performance enhancing but also good for the horses. They then set the trap and moved forward with a few test runs. The test runs must have gone very well because both trainers not only took the hook, but also they swallowed it!

This decision, on that day, forever changed the destiny of these two men and will likely prevent them from doing what they love for the rest of their lives! They didn't put much thought into the consequences of getting caught, and now there is Hell to pay! Not only have they hurt themselves but also their friends, family, and horses are feeling the pain. My hope for these two men is that they have learned a valuable lesson and are genuinely sorry for their actions. I hope they get closer to God and focus on their eternal destination! I hope they teach their family, friends, and anyone that will listen what they have learned.

I am not writing this story to discuss the two horse trainers. I am writing this to inform you that each and every one of us is being tempted just like they were. The only difference is the stakes are much higher! Your soul is on the line, and Hell is on the table. You will be tempted with the pleasures of this world, and the test runs that you are offered will go very well! The devil has done a masterful job in making the Ten Commandments dated and out of touch with our current society but, trust me, they aren't out of touch with God! What we all do on this short trip to earth will determine our final destination. God and Christ want you to join them in Heaven, and the devil wants your soul with him in Hell.

We are faced with a little bit of a tradeoff here. We are allowed to choose the short-term pleasures of this world and fall to temptation just like the horse trainers did. This will lead to many good times and fitting in with the rest of the crowd. You will have many friends to assure you that you are on the right track! The question you have to ask yourself is, are they really true friends or do they play for the devil's team? You will brush off any afterlife thoughts and not consider death until it comes knocking at the door. You will then face God and Judgement time and, just like the horse trainers, there will be Hell to pay.

I hope many of you reading this will spend a little time in the Bible, studying the teachings of Jesus Christ. His words are enjoyable and enlightening! Following God's plan and having faith in Christ will assure a victory over the devil and reserve a very special place in Heaven!

THE F-WORD

*For by thy words thou shalt be justified, and
by the words thou shalt be condemned.*

—Jesus Christ

If you look up some of the most spoken words in the English language, you come up with words like *the, that, have,* and *this.* I am starting to wonder where the f-word falls on the list. I am thinking that it's getting close to cracking the top ten. Hollywood has made cursing very popular, and it's very difficult to find a decent movie where the language is clean these days. Even regular TV has shocked me in recent years with the language and direction they are taking. They glamorize all kinds of sin and are leading our country in a very dark direction. Hollywood has made it very cool to curse! I recently played in a couple of golf outings, and while on the course, I kept hearing the f-word over and over again. Probably heard it thirty times during two rounds of golf. People definitely feel it is now part of the English language. Either way, it is a shame how society uses the ability to speak and, as Christ said, they will answer for it one day. From a golfing perspective I feel anyone who feels the need to say the F-word multiple times while playing a round might want to consider taking some lessons? From a biblical perspective, there are some very stern warnings that you might want to consider with your language.

One more thought for my golfing friends, I have a strong feeling in Heaven that you can dial up and play Augusta or Pine Valley any time you choose. Not so sure about tee times being available in Hell?

When I look for help with a subject, I try to rely on quotes from Christ. He had this to say regarding our words, "I tell you that on the day of judgment people will have to account for every careless word they speak." Cursing is not the only obstacle that we need to overcome with our language. We need to work harder on building people up and not tear them down! Words have great power. Choose them with compassion and try to help your fellow man!

Now let's discuss Heaven and Hell before we go. I have said in the past that I feel Heaven has a purity level that cannot be broken. I do not feel people are going to be firing off the f-word up in Heaven. I also feel a sin is a sin, and God looks at all sin through the same lens. I don't feel he looks at adultery, lying, or stealing any differently than he does murder. I feel you can be a great person, go to church every Sunday, donate to the homeless, and rescue animals every week. But if you continue sinning, you are not making it past the gates of Heaven! So now you have to ask yourself, is it worth the risk of going to Hell and disappointing your Creator to follow the devil's lead and teachings? I honestly don't feel he has your best interest at heart! One day, soon, Jesus Christ is going to send out his angels to gather the worthy men and women for a trip to Heaven. You do not want to be left behind due to following the devil and speaking foolish words.

The ability to speak is a blessing, honor, and privilege! Be thankful for the gift and use it wisely.

PRAYER FOR LEE TAYLOR

*For where two or three are gathered in
my name, there am I among them.*

—Jesus Christ

A very close friend, Lee Taylor, recently passed away. He was an avid racing fan and loved the racetrack! Before he passed, he asked if I would spread his ashes at the track. This was quite an honor for me. Lee's wife, Alice, was a devout Christian, but Lee never seemed quite sold on the Lord. While he was sick, I wanted to spend some time with him and discuss faith, but he was on very heavy medication and slipped into a coma quickly.

Today, with the family and friends gathered in one of the stands on the backside of the track, I walked out on the track with Lee's ashes. I asked the Lord if he would please open a door for Lee so he could be with his wife, Alice. I asked this through his Son, Jesus Christ, and then let the ashes fly! After everyone left, I was sitting at my desk at the barn and wondering if my prayer for Lee and Alice was heard. On my desk was a box of supplements for the horses. The company that sent the supplements included an insert with a Bible verse. Isaiah 38:16 says, "Lord, by such things people live; and my spirit finds life in them too. You restored me to health and let me live." I smiled after reading this and felt very good about Lee's final destination. Does anyone else believe that this rather large C stands for Christ? I believe he was present!

THE RETURN OF
JESUS CHRIST

—Jesus Christ

Over the years, thousands of people have attempted to predict a date for the end of times. Christ said that no one would know the exact date, but with his help, I believe we can pin it down and get close.

I am a man of faith and follow Jesus Christ. I also keep an eye on the devil and try my best to reveal his tactics and agenda whenever the opportunity presents itself. Every morning when I wake up, I spend a little time reading the Bible. I enjoy the Psalms and the Proverbs and put marks by certain scripture and then circle back and discuss them with my daughter.

Somedays, instead of picking out a chapter, I just flip the Bible open and see where we land. This is what happened a while back and is also what led me to write this story.

I was not thinking about the end of times and certainly wasn't looking for a date. Whenever people claimed to know a date, I quickly dismissed them because Christ said nobody would ever know, and that was good enough for me. Okay, so back to opening up my Bible; I opened it up and landed on Daniel chapter 12. Daniel is known as a prophet in the Bible. He was known for his wisdom, faith, character, and loyalty to God. Even when being put to death was on the table, he remained loyal and was thrown into the den of lions! An angel protected Daniel all through the night and, in the morning,

74

he was removed from the lion's den safe and sound! Daniel worked under four different kings and is one of the most revered men in the Bible! In other words, Daniel has a lot of credibility! The Bible verse that jumped out at me and might allow us to come up with a time frame is Daniel 12:11.

To put this in context, Daniel is asking either God, Christ, or an angel when the end of time is going to be. Verse 11 says, "And from the time that the daily sacrifice shall be taken away, and the abomination that make desolate set up, there shall be a thousand two hundred and ninety days." I believe that the taking away of the daily sacrifice could be in reference to the government stopping us all from going to church throughout the world. I also believe that the "abomination that make desolate" could very well be directly related to the coronavirus! Now let's get to Jesus Christ and his enlightening input.

As I have said in the past, when I quote the Bible, it is generally Christ that I quote! He is the most studied man in the world, and he is also who I respect above all others! The Daniel chapters were revealing, but I wanted to see if Christ ever shined any light on him. I did a search on Jesus Christ and the Prophet Daniel and, lo and behold, Jesus did speak of Daniel! Putting this in context, Jesus's disciples came to him at the Mount of Olives and, in Matthew 24:3, asked him, "Tell us, when shall these things be? And what shall be the sign of thy coming, and of the end of the world?"

Jesus went on to describe some of horrors that were going to happen, listing wars, famines, pestilence, and earthquakes, and then he brought up Daniel.

In Matthew 24:15, Jesus Christ says, "When you therefore shall see the abominations of desolation, spoken of by Daniel the Prophet stand in the holy place, (whoso readeth, let him understand:)."

I feel this is Jesus backing up Daniel's thoughts on the end of times and validating his 1,290 days after the daily sacrifice is taken away.

The Bible has you add 1,290 days to the date when we were stopped from going to church. I came up with around the middle of March for that and came up with October 2023 for the date of the return of Jesus Christ and the Rapture.

I feel Heaven is a very special place with family, friends and, hopefully, pets that I look forward to seeing again. I am eager to meet the Lord, Jesus Christ, and the angels that put up with me all these years and hope to ride my horse, Mountain, again. My hope is that having some time to weigh important options, many unbelievers will change teams, repent, and accept Jesus Christ as their personal Savior. They will accept the sacrifice that God and Christ made at the cross and choose to spend eternity in Heaven. You are at a fork in the road, people, and time is short! Don't wait on this! Choose Heaven by following God's plan, and we will see you on the high road.

Post script

I want to be clear that I do not know for sure that the abomination of desolation is connected to the coronavirus. I do feel the devil and evil people were involved, and common sense says it's possible. I am also not positive that the taking away the "daily sacrifice" was them stopping us from going to church but, once again, it makes sense and is possible. The other kicker that makes this an option is that Jesus Christ has not come yet, and the information I am using is coming from the Bible and Christ himself. Your call.

FORGIVENESS AND REVENGE

—Jesus Christ

I have struggled with the revenge thing over the years but have developed a plan that works well for me and is very successful.

Forgiveness is spoken of often in the Bible and unless you are a saint, you are in need of forgiveness. We have all made mistakes throughout our life but if we sincerely ask God for forgiveness, He is very happy to do so! God is also willing and very talented at providing revenge when it is deserved. Earlier in my life I used to try to take care of my own revenge. This rarely worked out well and on many occasions, I found out later on that my targets didn't deserve my anger and that the problem was simply a mistake or misunderstanding. I am extremely forgiving if bad things happen by accident or due to unintentional mistakes. I do however go sideways if I find out someone is purposely attempting harm to my family, friends, animals or myself. This also includes people in general that are being targeted by the devil's children with more frequency these days.

Revenge is also spoken of in the Bible and the bottom line is that God prefers to handle it Himself. He wants us to be forgiving and leave the revenge up to Him. I have come to find out over the years that He is very powerful and His discernment is perfect. He doesn't make mistakes.

So my plan works like this. When I feel someone has intentionally caused harm to the above mentioned group, I say a fairly simple prayer asking God to look into things and if deserved could He take the perfect revenge over said individuals. I then take a very deep breath, have a strong faith that he is going to take care of things and then let it go. This for me provides a sense of satisfaction that releases the strong urge for revenge. I feel it is going to be taken care of so the whole revenge thing is no longer my concern. This in turn allows me to do God's command and forgive the individuals that attempted to do harm. I find it amazing how the anger and burden is gone after I go through this process. I used to hold on to the anger and desire for revenge forever but now I can eliminate it in five minutes.

I highly recommend this for my friends and yes there is a catch. You have to play for God's team! Christ is the team manager, see him if you want to sign up…

THE VERY SPECIAL SWEATER

For the Father judgeth no man, but hath committed all judgment onto the Son.

—Jesus Christ

I went to the barn late this morning and checked on all the horses. Everything seemed in good order, so around nine, I headed off to church. The preacher man told this beautiful story of a visit he made to his childhood town in the dead of winter. He said he was walking through town, and outside of the old liquor store was a man sitting in a chair with his dog lying by his feet. As the preacher got closer, a cold breeze kicked up, and he watched this man stand up, take his sweater off, and wrap it around his dog! He mentioned the unconditional love the dog must have given him over the years! I drew a comparison to Christ dying on the cross and wrapping a sweater around all of us. Some of us take the sweater off and throw it on the ground, and others look up and are thankful. Me, I'm a sweater guy. I have enormous respect for what Jesus Christ did for us all!

Every one of us is on death row, and we need to make important choices before we die. We need to make the decision if we are going to focus on the world and play the devil's game, or are we going to choose God's plan and have faith in his Son and repent? Time goes by in the blink of an eye, and all those sins that the world now makes acceptable need to be cleared from your slate. If you want to spend eternity in Heaven, I highly recommend you put on the sweater!

A CONVERSATION WITH A BELIEVER IN GOD BUT NOT SOLD ON CHRIST

"I am the way, the truth, and the life. No man cometh unto the father, but by me."

—Jesus Christ

A while back I was speaking with a close friend of mine that had fallen on hard times. We all know how that goes when things keep hitting you one after another and you start to question yourself and what you did to deserve such devastation in your life? You ask your God with tears in your eyes to please help you understand what is going on and how to stop it. No answers are given and eventually you show anger towards God not realizing that he never received your message.

My conversation started by listening to the troubles that my friend was going through. Things were happening in sequence that were heartbreaking and he was understandably confused and extremely sad. I told him how sorry I was and then reached for a team that I felt was his best source for healing and bringing a sense of peace back to his life, the Father, Son and Holy Spirit. I asked him about his faith and where he stood with God? He pulled a chain up from around his neck and at the end was a beautiful cross. He expressed that he believed in God and that he prayed often. I then asked him about Jesus Christ and he seemed to stall a bit. He mentioned that he wasn't sold on Christ and mentioned that men wrote the Bible thus it could be flawed. He said when he prays he starts out directing the prayers to the True God and feels that they are getting where

83

they need to go. I then tried my best to explain my feelings on Jesus Christ and why his prayers might not be reaching God? I told him that most companies have a CEO that is the boss and makes most of the important decisions. I tried to show the chain of command and said the CEO will only be reached if the Vice President of the company feels the conversation or request is worthy of his attention. In other words, you have to go through the Vice President to get to the CEO. I then said that Jesus Christ himself said that the only way to reach out to God was to go through him. This would not make for a big change in my friend's prayer, it would be as simple as saying at the end of the prayer: "These things I ask through Jesus Christ." The question is did it sink in and how do I convince unbelievers?

Christ is the most studied man in the history of the world. The things he said are in red print in my Bible. In one of those sections of red, Christ explains to his disciples that many people are given a clear understanding of God but many are not. Jesus actually changed the way that he spoke to unbelievers and spoke in parables in an attempt to get through to them. He spent a lot of time and dedicated a lot of his service to saving the people that were blocked from knowing the truth. He knew it wasn't their fault and was doing what he could to save them. One of the last things he said on the Cross was a prayer request he sent up to God asking him to forgive the unbelievers that sent him to his death. "Please Father forgive them for they know not what they do." Considering the horrible suffering and pain that he had endured and for him to, with his last breath, still reach out and try and save the unbelievers, I see why God would want you to respectfully go through Jesus with your prayers to show him the honor and respect that he deserves.

So how did I do with my friend? Honestly I'm not sure? He seemed open to what I was saying but like many that I have spoken with in the past, something was holding him back. Something was trying to block him from taking the turn to Jesus Christ. Many people reading this post are also being blocked and have been their whole lives! My hope is that some of you hit your knees today and simply put in a prayer request asking Jesus Christ to speak to the Lord on your behalf and have Him reveal the Truth! This has never been more important than it is right now and I wish you all the best with your personal journey to Heaven!

I have chosen to finish my book here. I enjoyed writing it and hope you enjoyed reading it. Before I go, I want share with you a few more words from Jesus Christ and a few more from me.

*"I have not come to call the righteous,
but the sinners to repentance."*

I want everyone to know that I played for the devil's team for years. Committed every sin that I mentioned in this book, over and over again. I was fortunate and blessed to be shown some true miracles and was disciplined by God. I chose to change my life and destiny. I now work for God, Jesus Christ and the Holy Spirit within me. Life is so much better for me now and I hope in some way, you can find a way to change your destiny. May God Show You the Truth and the Way.

Glenn Thompson

N POOL

ABOUT THE AUTHOR

photo by Jan Taylor

Glenn Thompson is a man with a strong sense of faith that has had many collisions with the devil. His goal in life is to share his experiences and help people avoid the traps that the devil has set before them. He hopes to meet people in Heaven that have strengthened their faith with his book and chosen Heaven over Hell.